52-WEEK FEELINGS JOURNAL FOR TEENS

DAILY REFLECTION, EXPRESSION, AND 5-MINUTE MINDFULNESS MOMENTS

Tiffany Ruelaz, PhD, LPC, CDBT

ROCKRIDGE
PRESS

D1738517

THESE FEELINGS BELONG TO

_____

FEELINGS, FEELINGS, AND MORE FEELINGS

Welcome to the *52-Week Feelings Journal for Teens*! Being a teenager comes with a LOT of feelings, and all you want is for someone to get it, to help you figure this stuff out. Whether you have been feeling anxious, sad, or angry, you and your feelings are completely normal. Think of emotions like little toddlers when they want a toy at the store. If they get ignored, they become louder and louder, making it nearly impossible to focus on anything else. However, if you recognize why they are upset, and work with each one (without always giving them everything they want), life will feel much easier. Feelings do not have to seem so awful, intense, or overwhelming that you want to hide from or bury them. Everyone manages their emotions a little differently, and that's okay.

This journal provides you with 52 weeks of prompts, mind-fulness practices, and feelings challenges to help you feel more comfortable understanding and expressing your emotions. There are so many things you can do to work with your emotions, and journaling is a great way to start!

HOW TO USE THIS JOURNAL

This journal has many great tools for you to use, starting with some tips for journaling and ways to build your vocabulary so you can better describe your feelings. You will have space to journal every day for 52 weeks—just circle the letter of the day you are on and start writing. Every week, you will have a "feelings theme" to write about that will help you learn about your emotions and how to experience and express them. Alongside each weekly prompt is a challenge to help you put what you've learned into practice. You will also be able to reflect on and track how often you complete the 5-Minute Mindfulness tasks. There is a table of contents at the back of the book for the Feelings Challenges and 5-Minute Mindfulness exercises, too, so you can return to any challenge or exercise any time you want. If you stay consistent and have fun, you will be able to look back on your year and see how far you've come!

JOURNALING TIPS

When you journal consistently, you get to know your emotions and learn how to manage them much better. Here are some tips to help you get started.

1. Create a routine for yourself. Choose the time of day you usually have free time, and try to write at that same time each day.

2. Set a reminder for yourself to journal, then change your reminder every month. For example, month 1 could be a daily phone reminder and month 2 could be a sticky note on the bathroom mirror.

3. Stay focused on YOU and your feelings, not those of some-one else (unless prompted).

4. Use "I" statements to focus on your feelings. For me, my "I" statement looks like this: "I feel excited that you chose to journal here because I want to help." Fill in the blanks with your own words.

5. If you have a busy week, take a picture of the pages and "journal" in a note app on your phone—but don't make this a habit. Instead, try to devote the necessary time to journaling on paper.

6. If you aren't sure what something means, look it up. You can search online to understand certain feeling words or concepts that you want to know more about.

7. Make time to go back to previous topics and read what you wrote. This can help you consistently grow.

FEELINGS CHART

The chart on pages viii and ix is a tool to help you identify which feelings you might be having in a given moment. Use the chart to build your "feelings vocabulary" as you move through this journal.

FEAR		HAPPINESS		ANGER	
Rejected	Alienated Worthless Inadequate Shunned Excluded	Joyful	Jubilant Thrilled Ecstatic Radiant Elated	Hurt	Embarrassed Put Down Devastated Shattered Crushed
Submissive	Insignificant Obedient Subdued Passive	Interested	Curious Amused Inquisitive Attentive	Threatened	Unsafe Exposed Jealous Vulnerable
Insecure	Inferior Timid Apprehensive Unsure	Proud	Dignified Important Confident Self-assured	Hateful	Sickened Resentful Violated Bitter
Anxious	Nervous Overwhelmed Disturbed Distressed	Accepted	Respected Endorsed Fulfilled Welcomed	Mad	Furious Distraught Enraged Upset
Scared	Frightened Terrified Alarmed Panicky	Powerful	Dominant Commanding Courageous Dynamic	Aggressive	Provoked Controlling Hostile Argumentative
Worried	Tense Distracted Fearful Stressed	Peaceful	Hopeful Calm Loving Gentle	Frustrated	Infuriated Agitated Irritated Concerned
		Intimate	Playful Tender Sensitive Cozy	Distant	Withdrawn Aloof Suspicious Standoffish
		Optimistic	Positive Upbeat Open Cheerful	Critical	Skeptical Demanding Sarcastic Scolding
		Arrogant	Condescending Boastful Bossy Cocky	Indignant	Annoyed Outraged Livid Incensed
		Appreciative	Admiring Obliged Pleased Grateful	Offended	Insulted Slighted Disrespected Humiliated

DISGUST			SADNESS		SURPRISE	
Disapproving	Judgmental Critical Loathsome Contemptuous	Guilty	Remorseful Mortified Ashamed Responsible	Startled	Shocked Taken Aback Dismayed Horrified
Disappointed	Discouraged Disheartened Wretched Disillusioned	Abandoned	Ignored Neglected Victimized Forgotten	Confused	Disconcerted Disoriented Perplexed Stunned
Awful	Nauseated Disgusted Detestable Abhorrent	Despondent	Powerless Destroyed Miserable Hopeless	Amazed	Astonished Flabbergasted Awed Dumbfounded
Avoidant	In Denial Hesitant Repelled Withdrawn	Depressed	Numb Resigned Empty Somber	Excited	Eager Passionate Energetic Enthusiastic
		Lonely	Reclusive Detached Isolated Ostracized		
		Bored	Apathetic Neutral Indifferent Disinterested		

INTRODUCTION TO FEELINGS

What do you believe about your emotions? Choose a different feeling to write about each day, including the beliefs you have about that feeling.

MTWTF ___/___/___

_____

_____

MTWTF ___/___/___

_____

_____

MTWTF ___/___/___

_____

_____

MTWTF ___/___/___

_____

_____

MTWTF ___/___/___

_____

_____

_____

Identify and describe three emotions you had today and why you had them.

SS ___/___/___

_____

_____

_____

_____

_____

_____

_____

"'You're going to be happy,' said life. 'But first, I'll make you strong.'"

–Paulo Coelho

Using the Feelings Chart on pages viii and ix, write about a situation that happened this week. Identify your feelings and how they affected you.

SS ___/___/___

_____

_____

_____

_____

_____

_____

_____

FEELINGS CHALLENGE: NOTICE THE FEELINGS!

Try to count how many feelings you experience on the Feelings Chart (pages viii and ix) in one day.

5 MINUTES TO CALM

Step 1: Find a quiet place without distractions. Set an alarm for 5 minutes. Take a deep breath and close your eyes.

Step 2: Think about what happened today.

Step 3: Identify one emotion and let yourself feel it without pushing it away.

Step 4: Once the alarm goes off, take another deep breath and open your eyes.

Pick one emotion that you often feel when interacting with others. Write about a time this emotion helped you communicate your needs.

MTWTF   __/__/__

_____

_____

MTWTF   __/__/__

_____

_____

MTWTF   __/__/__

_____

_____

MTWTF   __/__/__

_____

_____

MTWTF   __/__/__

_____

_____

_____

How has an emotion you've communicated to someone helped you solve a conflict or a miscommunication? Did communicating that feeling help the other person understand what you were experiencing in that moment?

SS   __/__/__

_____

_____

_____

_____

_____

_____

_____

"The single biggest problem in communication is the illusion that it has taken place."

—George Bernard Shaw

Think of a time when you won something or accomplished something. How did you let people know how you felt?

SS   __/__/__

_____

_____

_____

_____

_____

_____

_____

FEELINGS CHALLENGE: SHOW GRATITUDE!

Tell a friend how much you value them and why.

5 MINUTES TO HAPPINESS

Step 1: Find a quiet place to reflect.

Step 2: Think about a time when you felt very happy while with a family member. Notice how your body feels right now.

Step 3: What face are you making? What would this face communicate to the people around you?

Step 4: Be mindful of how your happiness impacts the happiness of others.

Write about a time when you felt as if your emotions controlled you. Describe what you did to work through it and feel better.

MTWTF   __/__/__

_____

_____

_____

MTWTF   __/__/__

_____

_____

_____

MTWTF   __/__/__

_____

_____

_____

MTWTF   __/__/__

_____

_____

_____

MTWTF   __/__/__

_____

_____

_____

Write about how it feels to talk to a good friend.

SS ___/___/___

"The only way to change someone's mind is to connect with them from the heart."

—Rasheed Ogunlaru

Write about a time when you felt understood by someone else. Maybe they went through an experience similar to yours or had a similar family dynamic. How did it feel to be understood?

SS ___/___/___

FEELINGS CHALLENGE: GET CONNECTED!

Notice when you feel happy or excited and express it to others in the moment.

5 MINUTES TO EMPATHY

Step 1: Find a place to sit and watch people. Set a timer for 5 minutes.

Step 2: Watch a specific person and imagine that you are living their life in that moment.

Step 3: Reflect on how you would be feeling if you were them, without judgment, until the timer goes off.

WHAT MOTIVATES YOU?

Write about what you accomplished this week. What feelings helped motivate you?

MTWTF ___/___/___

MTWTF ___/___/___

MTWTF ___/___/___

MTWTF ___/___/___

MTWTF ___/___/___

Sometimes anger, frustration, or annoyance can motivate us to be assertive. Write about a time you told someone what you needed.

SS   __/__/__

_____

_____

_____

_____

_____

_____

"All our dreams can come true if we have the courage to pursue them."

—Walt Disney

Think of a time this week when you felt happy. What led you to feel that way? Did you talk to friends or family? Did you play games or spend time with a pet? Write about your experience feeling motivated by happiness.

SS   __/__/__

_____

_____

_____

_____

_____

_____

FEELINGS CHALLENGE: GET MOTIVATED!

Choose one new activity you have been wanting to do, then go do it. Notice how you feel before, during, and after the activity.

5 MINUTES TO CALM

Step 1: Set a timer for 3 minutes.

Step 2: Close your eyes and think about what makes you happy and makes you feel good.

Step 3: Picture yourself working hard to get the things you want.

Step 4: Once the timer goes off, take a deep breath, open your eyes, and use the motivators you pictured to help you succeed.

Reasonable thoughts are driven by facts; emotional thoughts are driven by feelings. Write about a time you balanced thoughts and feelings when making a decision.

MTWTF   ___/___/___

_____
_____
_____

MTWTF   ___/___/___

_____
_____
_____

MTWTF   ___/___/___

_____
_____
_____

MTWTF   ___/___/___

_____
_____
_____

MTWTF   ___/___/___

_____
_____
_____

Feelings can act as red flags or alarms that help us pay closer attention to a situation. Describe a time when your feelings helped you notice something important.

SS   __/__/__

"Balanced emotions are crucial to intuitive decision-making."

—Michael Eisner

Write about a decision you had to make this week and what feelings you had about it. (It could be what to wear, what to eat, or something more complicated.)

SS   __/__/__

FEELINGS CHALLENGE: BE WISE!

Use a balance of reasonable thoughts and emotions to choose what to focus on in your free time.

5 MINUTES TO CONFIDENCE

Step 1: Find a quiet place to sit and think.

Step 2: Think about a decision you had to make recently. Reflect on what you thought was "rational" or "logical" about that decision.

Step 3: Reflect on what you felt you wanted or what your gut told you to do about the decision. Were your thoughts in line with your feelings? Reflect on your decision.

Step 4: Give yourself credit for noticing the difference between your thoughts and feelings.

STYLES OF THINKING

Changing how we think about things can help us feel happier. Write about some thoughts you had today and how those thoughts made you feel.

MTWTF   __/__/__

_____

_____

MTWTF   __/__/__

_____

_____

MTWTF   __/__/__

_____

_____

MTWTF   __/__/__

_____

_____

MTWTF   __/__/__

_____

_____

Focusing only on negative things can greatly impact our mood.
Write about all of the positive things that happened today.

SS   __/__/__

_____

_____

_____

_____

_____

_____

"Feelings are something you have;
not something you are."

—Shannon L. Alder

Sometimes we believe we are our emotions. For example, "I feel like
a bad friend, therefore I am a bad friend." Write about a time this
happened to you, how you felt about it, and how you dealt with it.

SS   __/__/__

_____

_____

_____

_____

_____

_____

FEELINGS CHALLENGE: TALLY THE THOUGHTS!

For one day, keep track of how often you only focus on the negatives in a situation. Give yourself credit for simply noticing.

5 MINUTES TO HAPPINESS

Step 1: Find a quiet place to sit. Set a timer for 3 minutes.

Step 2: Think about a positive memory. Play it in your mind like a movie.

Step 3: Notice what emotions come up and allow yourself to feel them all over again.

Step 4: Once the memory is done playing, take those positive feelings with you and let yourself feel happy!

TRIGGERING FEELINGS

When we experience something that causes us physical or mental pain or anxiety, that's a trigger. Notice any triggers you have and write about how you feel when they happen.

MTWTF ___/___/___

_____

_____

MTWTF ___/___/___

_____

_____

MTWTF ___/___/___

_____

_____

MTWTF ___/___/___

_____

_____

MTWTF ___/___/___

_____

_____

Write about a time you helped someone when they felt triggered. How did you help them?

SS ___/___/___

_____

_____

_____

_____

_____

_____

_____

"When dealing with people, remember you are not dealing with creatures of logic, but with creatures of emotion."

—Dale Carnegie

Listening to music is one way to manage triggered feelings. Write about a time you felt triggered and what you did to overcome the feeling.

SS ___/___/___

_____

_____

_____

_____

_____

_____

_____

Write a letter to someone you care about, telling them all the reasons you enjoy spending time with them.

5 MINUTES TO CALM

Step 1: Picture a square in front of you and imagine tracing one side during each of the following steps. Breathe in through your nose for 4 seconds, going up the left side of the square in your mind.

Step 2: Hold your breath for 4 seconds, going across the top of the square in your mind.

Step 3: Exhale through your mouth for 4 seconds, going down the other side of the square. Hold your breath for 4 seconds, completing the tracing of the square.

Step 4: Repeat this 4 times, going all around the square. If you do this when you feel stressed, it will help you feel calmer.

The average teen needs 9 to 10 hours of sleep each night. Note how many hours of sleep you get each night this week. How do you feel each day?

MTWTF   __/__/__

_____

_____

_____

MTWTF   __/__/__

_____

_____

_____

MTWTF   __/__/__

_____

_____

_____

MTWTF   __/__/__

_____

_____

_____

MTWTF   __/__/__

_____

_____

_____

Do you get 9 to 10 hours of sleep on average? If not, how can you change your routine? If you already do, how can you stay consistent?

SS   __/__/__

_____

_____

_____

_____

_____

_____

_____

"As the night gets dark, let your worries fade. Sleep peacefully knowing you've done all you can do for today."

—Roald Dahl

Sleeping too much (11+ hours) can impact our mood as much as sleeping too little. Write about a time you overslept and how you felt physically and mentally.

SS   __/__/__

_____

_____

_____

_____

_____

_____

_____

FEELINGS CHALLENGE: GET READY FOR BED!

Challenge yourself to turn off all screens 30 minutes before you go to bed, 3 times this week.

5 MINUTES TO CALM

Step 1: Lie down in your bed with the lights out or dimmed.

Step 2: Inhale through your nose for 4 seconds.

Step 3: Hold your breath for 7 seconds.

Step 4: Slowly breathe out through your mouth for 8 seconds.

Step 5: Repeat this for about 5 minutes or until you fall asleep.

THOUGHTS AND FEELINGS

Our thoughts can really impact our mood. Write down what you're thinking about right now and how those thoughts are making you feel.

MTWTF   __/__/__

_____

_____

MTWTF   __/__/__

_____

_____

MTWTF   __/__/__

_____

_____

MTWTF   __/__/__

_____

_____

MTWTF   __/__/__

_____

_____

Write about a time you had to work in a group. What were your thoughts about the other people's work styles? How did those thoughts affect how you felt about them?

SS ___/___/___

"Positive thoughts generate positive feelings and attract positive life experiences."

—Mae West

Think of a time when you felt pressured to complete a task. What thoughts did you have about the task? How did your thoughts affect your emotions?

SS ___/___/___

FEELINGS CHALLENGE: FEEL THE MUSIC!

Listen to a genre of music that you haven't heard before (e.g., Polka, techno, country, rap). Notice what thoughts and feelings come up about this new music.

5 MINUTES TO CALM

Step 1: Sit in a comfortable position and close your eyes.

Step 2: Visualize yourself watching a train go by.

Step 3: Take each thought that enters your mind and put it on a train car. Let the thoughts flow at their own pace, and if you get distracted, simply bring yourself back to watching the train and putting each distracting thought on one of the cars.

Step 4: Once you feel fewer thoughts cluttering your mind, take a deep breath and open your eyes.

Have you ever felt "hangry" and then eaten a great meal that made you feel better? Write about a time when food helped you feel better.

MTWTF ___/___/___

_____

_____

MTWTF ___/___/___

_____

_____

MTWTF ___/___/___

_____

_____

MTWTF ___/___/___

_____

_____

MTWTF ___/___/___

_____

_____

Write about a time you ate a good meal with your family. How did it make you feel?

SS ___/___/___

_____

_____

_____

_____

_____

_____

"A balanced life is like a three-legged stool. Each leg—nutrition, fitness, and wellness—is necessary and supports the other."

—Ellie Krieger

Write about your experience with food in general. What foods do you eat that make your body feel good?

SS ___/___/___

_____

_____

_____

_____

_____

_____

FEELINGS CHALLENGE: EAT UP!

Use a balance of reasonable thoughts and emotions to choose what you will eat for one meal this week.

5 MINUTES TO GRATITUDE

Step 1: Pick a piece of your favorite fruit to eat.

Step 2: Before eating it, close your eyes and feel it in your hands. Notice its texture and size. Is it rough or smooth?

Step 3: Smell the fruit.

Step 4: Put it against your tongue and notice the flavors as you begin to eat the fruit.

Step 5: Notice how much it takes to feel satisfied or full without overeating.

Describe an event that made you feel sad, mad, or frustrated. On a scale of 0 to 10, how intense were those feelings? How did you react to the event?

MTWTF ___/___/___

_____

_____

MTWTF ___/___/___

_____

_____

MTWTF ___/___/___

_____

_____

MTWTF ___/___/___

_____

_____

MTWTF ___/___/___

_____

_____

_____

Write about a time when you felt really happy when interacting with people. What was your body language like at the time? Describe your tone of voice.

SS ___/___/___

_____

_____

_____

_____

_____

_____

_____

"Unleash in the right time and place before you explode at the wrong time and place."

—Oli Anderson

Write about a time when your behavior positively or negatively impacted people around you. How did you feel after finding out how they felt (grateful, afraid, relieved)?

SS ___/___/___

_____

_____

_____

_____

_____

_____

FEELINGS CHALLENGE: BLOW BUBBLES!

Go blow bubbles with friends. You are never too old to blow bubbles, and doing so is great for calming our bodies.

5 MINUTES TO CALM

Step 1: Imagine you are holding a ball that contains the source of all your negative feelings.

Step 2: Notice what it feels like to hold the ball. Let the ball go, bounce the ball, or put it down.

Step 3: If you choose to bounce the ball, picture the negative energy flying out of the ball as it bounces. If you choose to hold the ball, decide what you will do with the negative energy inside. If you put it down, or let it go, you do something with the negative energy another time.

Step 4: Take a deep breath and return back to neutral energy, without the ball in your hands.

EXERCISE

When you exercise, happiness chemicals called endorphins are released in your brain. Write about the physical activities you like to do and how you feel when you do them.

MTWTF ___/___/___

MTWTF ___/___/___

MTWTF ___/___/___

MTWTF ___/___/___

MTWTF ___/___/___

Write about a time you used exercise to feel better.

SS   __/__/__

"Exercise should be regarded as tribute to the heart."

—Gene Tunney

Think about how much fun you had at recess when you were younger. How did playing outside make you feel?

SS   __/__/__

FEELINGS CHALLENGE: CREATIVE EXERCISE!

Make up your own active 20-minute indoor or outdoor game to play with friends or siblings.

5 MINUTES TO HAPPINESS

Step 1: Go for a 5-minute walk outside.

Step 2: Notice any plants, birds, and/or people you see. How do they interact with you (if at all)?

Step 3: How do you feel being outdoors?

Step 4: Take note of any other feelings you have. Mindfully observe your surroundings...

Step 5: Congratulate yourself for being mindful and exercising at the same time!

ACHIEVING GOALS

Helpful goals are SMART: **s**pecific, **m**easurable, **a**chievable, **r**ealistic, and have a **t**ime frame. Describe goals you have that fit these criteria. How do these goals make you feel?

MTWTF ___/___/___

_____

_____

MTWTF ___/___/___

_____

_____

MTWTF ___/___/___

_____

_____

MTWTF ___/___/___

_____

_____

MTWTF ___/___/___

_____

_____

_____

Make a plan for how to achieve your next big goal. Identify a time when you can start working toward it.

SS ___/___/___

"If my mind can conceive it and my heart can believe it—then I can achieve it."

—Muhammad Ali

What feelings will help motivate you to achieve your next goal? What feelings might get in your way, and how can you overcome them? Use the Feelings Chart on pages viii and ix.

SS ___/___/___

FEELINGS CHALLENGE: MAKE A VISION BOARD!

Find things online that represent your short-term goals. Put them together in an image such as a collage, and make it your screen saver or phone background.

5 MINUTES TO CONFIDENCE

Step 1: Find a quiet place to sit. Set an alarm for 5 minutes. Take a deep breath and close your eyes.

Step 2: Think about what your life might look like one year from now. Think about how much you have grown physically and emotionally in the last year.

Step 3: Now think about what you want to be doing next year. Think about what you have to do to accomplish that goal. Then imagine yourself accomplishing it!

Step 4: Take a deep breath and open your eyes.

Self-esteem is how you think about yourself. Describe one feeling you have when looking in the mirror each day this week.

MTWTF   __/__/__

_____

_____

MTWTF   __/__/__

_____

_____

MTWTF   __/__/__

_____

_____

MTWTF   __/__/__

_____

_____

MTWTF   __/__/__

_____

_____

Many people criticize the way they look, and doing so hurts their self-esteem. List three things you like about the way you look and why.

SS   __/__/__

_____

_____

_____

_____

_____

_____

"The only person you will live your entire life with is yourself."

—Judy A. Killian

Write about your journey with physical self-esteem and how it has affected you.

SS   __/__/__

_____

_____

_____

_____

_____

_____

_____

FEELINGS CHALLENGE: BEAUTY AND THE FILTER

Find a picture of a celebrity and try to find all the places the photo was altered. Remember that we are all beautiful without the Photoshop and filters, too!

5 MINUTES TO CONFIDENCE

Step 1: Take one picture of yourself without any filters.

Step 2: Compliment yourself as if you were your own best friend.

SELF-LOVE OR SELFISH?

Watching your favorite show, reading a good book, and calling a friend are examples of self-love, and they can positively impact our emotions. What do you do to take care of yourself?

MTWTF   __/__/__

_____

_____

MTWTF   __/__/__

_____

_____

MTWTF   __/__/__

_____

_____

MTWTF   __/__/__

_____

_____

MTWTF   __/__/__

_____

_____

_____

Society thinks it's "bad" to be selfish. But taking care of yourself is not selfish! Write about a time you felt selfish when you were doing something just for yourself.

SS   __/__/__

"You can't pour from an empty cup. Take care of yourself first."

—Anonymous

Our relationships with others improve when we take care of ourselves. Write about the things that make you feel happy and how they positively affect your relationships.

SS   __/__/__

FEELINGS CHALLENGE: DO IT FOR YOU!

Think of what makes you the happiest. Take time to do something you really love this week.

5 MINUTES TO CALM

Step 1: Get up early in the morning and watch the sunrise.

Step 2: Allow yourself to feel close to nature. Remember that nature is all around us; you can connect with nature simply by looking up at the sky wherever you are.

Step 3: Notice what you are thinking and feeling.

Step 4: Go experience your day, feeling calm and connected to the Earth.

GIVE YOURSELF CREDIT!

Giving yourself credit is important for managing feelings and improving your mood. Describe, in detail, something you did well today.

MTWTF ___/___/___

_____

_____

_____

MTWTF ___/___/___

_____

_____

_____

MTWTF ___/___/___

_____

_____

_____

MTWTF ___/___/___

_____

_____

_____

MTWTF ___/___/___

_____

_____

_____

One big accomplishment I am really proud of is . . .

SS   __/__/__

_____

_____

_____

_____

_____

_____

"Nothing can bring you peace but yourself."
—Ralph Waldo Emerson

Describe the "small" accomplishments you had this week and how you feel looking back on them. An accomplishment can be as small as remembering to floss or turning in homework on time.

SS   __/__/__

_____

_____

_____

_____

_____

_____

_____

FEELINGS CHALLENGE: "WAY TO GO" LIST

Make a list of your accomplishments from the last couple of weeks. Share this list with a family member or a friend.

5 MINUTES TO CONFIDENCE

Step 1: Write down a SMART goal you want to work toward (see page 37 for a refresher on SMART goals).

Step 2: Think of one small step you can take toward achieving your goal, and do that today.

Step 3: Notice and appreciate your ability to take steps toward your goal.

Step 4: Tell yourself, "I followed through!" or "I'm proud of myself for trying."

BEING MINDFUL

Be mindful and notice the world around you by using any or all of your five senses—sight, smell, taste, touch, and hearing. Name some ways you are mindful.

MTWTF　　　　　　　　　　　　　　　　　　　　　__/__/__

_____

_____

MTWTF　　　　　　　　　　　　　　　　　　　　　__/__/__

_____

_____

MTWTF　　　　　　　　　　　　　　　　　　　　　__/__/__

_____

_____

MTWTF　　　　　　　　　　　　　　　　　　　　　__/__/__

_____

_____

MTWTF　　　　　　　　　　　　　　　　　　　　　__/__/__

_____

_____

If you have trouble with anger, anxiety, or focusing, being mindful can help you slow down and regroup. How can you use mindfulness to improve your life?

SS ___/___/___

_____

_____

_____

_____

_____

_____

"Wherever you are, be there totally."

—Eckhart Tolle

The purpose of being mindful is to help yourself feel calm, focused, and present in the moment. When do you feel most at peace?

SS ___/___/___

_____

_____

_____

_____

_____

_____

_____

FEELINGS CHALLENGE: BE MINDFUL

Download an app or find a website that helps you practice mindfulness. Set reminders to use exercises provided in the app three times each week.

5 MINUTES TO CALM

Step 1: Sit in a place where you feel very comfortable (inside or outside), and set an alarm for 3 minutes.

Step 2: Use as many senses as you can to notice what you are experiencing. Breathe in the air, look around, listen to the sounds, and notice any physical sensations in the body as well as the temperature around you.

Step 3: Continue being as mindful as you can throughout the day.

Patterns help us make judgments quickly and keep us safe, but sometimes they negatively impact us, too. Write about a time you jumped to conclusions.

MTWTF   __/__/__

_____

_____

_____

MTWTF   __/__/__

_____

_____

_____

MTWTF   __/__/__

_____

_____

_____

MTWTF   __/__/__

_____

_____

_____

MTWTF   __/__/__

_____

_____

_____

Our brain uses patterns to help us prepare for the future. Think of a time your brain used past experiences to help you prepare for an upcoming event.

SS   __/__/__

"When you hear hoofbeats behind you, don't expect to see a zebra."

—Theodore Woodward

Sometimes we think about the worst-case scenario even when a positive outcome is more likely to occur. Write about a time when you thought something wouldn't go well, but it did.

SS   __/__/__

FEELINGS CHALLENGE: GET THE PATTERNS!

Our brain's patterns can either help us or hinder us. Look up some riddles online and try to answer them. See how close you can come.

5 MINUTES TO EMPATHY

Step 1: Set a timer for 5 minutes and walk around your house, observing your family.

Step 2: Notice what they are doing versus what you expected them to be doing.

Step 3: Pay close attention to the small details: what they are doing and how they look doing it.

GET MOVING ON MOTIVATION

Motivation can be hard to maintain. Write about one time in the last week when you felt motivated and one time you didn't. What was the difference (aside from the motivation level)?

MTWTF _/_/_

_____

_____

_____

MTWTF _/_/_

_____

_____

_____

MTWTF _/_/_

_____

_____

_____

MTWTF _/_/_

_____

_____

_____

MTWTF _/_/_

_____

_____

_____

Make a list of things that motivate you to get up in the morning, then add the reasons they motivate you. For example, they make you feel happy, energized, or good about yourself.

SS   __/__/__

"Happiness is not something readymade, it comes from your own actions."

—Dalai Lama

Describe a task that you hate doing and why. How does it feel when you complete the task? What motivates you to complete it?

SS   __/__/__

Set your alarm 15 minutes earlier, three days in a row this week. Get out of bed when it rings.

5 MINUTES TO HAPPINESS

Step 1: Find a task that you want to accomplish.

Step 2: Put on your favorite music.

Step 3: Dance or sing while completing your task. Then celebrate finishing it!

TRY THE OPPOSITE

Sometimes we get stuck in a cycle of intense emotions. When you're feeling sad or frustrated, try feeling the opposite emotion—happy or peaceful. Write about a hard time and what you did to feel better.

MTWTF ___/___/___

MTWTF ___/___/___

MTWTF ___/___/___

MTWTF ___/___/___

MTWTF ___/___/___

Write down all the feelings you are experiencing right now, and then list their opposites. Use the Feelings Chart on pages viii and ix to help.

SS ___/___/___

_____

_____

_____

_____

_____

_____

_____

"So many things can make you happy. Don't focus too much on things that make you sad."

—Unknown

Write about the things that cheer you up when you are feeling sad, angry, or hurt.

SS ___/___/___

_____

_____

_____

_____

_____

_____

_____

FEELINGS CHALLENGE: SOMETHING NEW

Getting out of your comfort zone and doing something new is important for growth. Go say hello to someone you haven't talked to at school or find a pen pal from a different town or city.

5 MINUTES TO GRATITUDE

Step 1: Go to a quiet place and sit.

Step 2: Identify the emotions you're feeling (use the Feelings Chart on pages viii and ix for help).

Step 3: Allow yourself to understand why the emotions are there. What are the opposite emotions you could be feeling instead?

"SHOULD" VERSUS "WANT"

Pressure can be a great motivator. However, it can also lead us to feel trapped and resentful. Write about a time someone told you "You should . . . " and what you wanted to do instead.

MTWTF   __/__/__

_____

_____

_____

MTWTF   __/__/__

_____

_____

_____

MTWTF   __/__/__

_____

_____

_____

MTWTF   __/__/__

_____

_____

_____

MTWTF   __/__/__

_____

_____

_____

"You should" statements create unnecessary pressure from outside sources (family, peers, and society), making it hard to set boundaries. What does pressure feel like to you?

ss ___/___/___

"I'm not in this world to live up to your standards, and you're not in this world to live up to mine."

—Fritz Perls

It can be hard to live up to other people's standards. What are your standards for yourself, and where do you think they came from?

ss ___/___/___

FEELINGS CHALLENGE: SHOULD YOU?

Listen to your thoughts throughout the day. Any time you think the word "should," replace it with the word "want" and see if the sentence is still true.

5 MINUTES TO CONFIDENCE

Step 1: Find a quiet place to sit and set a timer for 5 minutes.

Step 2: Picture what you want to do after this exercise. See yourself doing the task.

Step 3: Now envision something getting in the way of doing what you want. Think about a way around the obstacle and see yourself resolving the issue. Feel confident that you can accomplish what you want to do!

TRUST

Trusting yourself can be hard when you are unsure of who you are. Write about what makes you a trustworthy person.

MTWTF   __/__/__

_____

_____

MTWTF   __/__/__

_____

_____

MTWTF   __/__/__

_____

_____

MTWTF   __/__/__

_____

_____

MTWTF   __/__/__

_____

_____

_____

Trust is one of the most important parts of any relationship. Write about whom you trust the most and why.

SS ___/___/___

_____

_____

_____

_____

_____

_____

"Hate is not the first enemy of love. Fear is. It destroys your ability to trust."

—Unknown

Write about a time you trusted someone and they broke your trust. How did you feel after it happened? How did you (or could you) overcome it?

SS ___/___/___

_____

_____

_____

_____

_____

_____

FEELINGS CHALLENGE: TRUST AND SECRETS

Building trust creates good relationships, but it can be hard to do. Tell a friend or a family member a secret about yourself.

5 MINUTES TO CONFIDENCE

Step 1: Think about an experience in which a friend trusted you and you were there for them.

Step 2: Remember the emotions you felt. Why do you think you felt them?

Step 3: Repeat to yourself, "I am trustworthy, and I can choose whom to trust."

CREATIVITY

Creativity comes from our emotions and allows us to connect to others. Creativity is in everyone, even if it's not obvious at first glance. Describe ways in which you are creative.

MTWTF ___/___/___

_____

_____

MTWTF ___/___/___

_____

_____

MTWTF ___/___/___

_____

_____

MTWTF ___/___/___

_____

_____

MTWTF ___/___/___

_____

_____

_____

When we are feeling upset, it can be difficult to calm ourselves down. Expressing creativity is a great way to help. List five creative things you can do to help yourself feel better when you are upset.

SS ___/___/___

"Conformity is the jailer of freedom, and the enemy of growth."

—John F. Kennedy

When we try to be like everyone else, we can lose some of our creativity. Write about a time this week when you felt unique.

SS ___/___/___

FEELINGS CHALLENGE: BE CREATIVE!

Choose something creative to do three times this week for 20 minutes each time, whether it is making art or music or doing a new exercise.

5 MINUTES TO HAPPINESS

Step 1: Grab a piece of paper and a pencil (or colored pencils).

Step 2: Draw a spiral. Don't worry about how perfect it looks. Then make staggered lines within your spiral.

Step 3: Color the different sections created by the overlapping lines and admire your work once you're done.

All emotions have a purpose. Some emotions, like anger and frustration, protect us from more vulnerable emotions like hurt, pain, and fear. Write about the things that make you feel vulnerable.

MTWTF   __/__/__

_____

_____

MTWTF   __/__/__

_____

_____

MTWTF   __/__/__

_____

_____

MTWTF   __/__/__

_____

_____

MTWTF   __/__/__

_____

_____

_____

Describe what happens when anger and frustration (the protector emotions) take over when you are feeling vulnerable.

SS
_/_/_

_____

_____

_____

_____

_____

_____

"Angry is just sad's bodyguard."

—Liza Palmer

Hurt, pain, and fear often need protector emotions because they can be hard to feel. Write about a time this week when you felt afraid and what you did to feel better.

SS
_/_/_

_____

_____

_____

_____

_____

_____

Watch the movie *Inside Out* and pay attention to which emotions try to protect the others.

5 MINUTES TO CALM

Step 1: Think about a situation that makes you feel a little upset and notice which emotions come up for you first.

Step 2: Picture those emotions as energy and bring that energy into a ball that you hold in your hands.

Step 3: Now, picture a healing light flowing through your body and hitting the ball, until the ball is gone.

MAGNIFYING AND MINIMIZING

When we make a situation bigger (magnify) or smaller (minimize) than it is, we affect the intensity of our emotions. Write about some recent times when this happened.

MTWTF ___/___/___

_____

_____

MTWTF ___/___/___

_____

_____

MTWTF ___/___/___

_____

_____

MTWTF ___/___/___

_____

_____

MTWTF ___/___/___

_____

_____

The best way to overcome magnifying/minimizing is to look at the facts. Describe only the facts of a situation. How does this feel?

SS   __/__/__

"We are created for adventure, and if we cannot find one, we start blowing things out of proportion so it feels like we have one."

—John Eldredge

It's okay to feel sadness or happiness without overthinking it. Describe a recent experience you had with feeling an emotion just as it was, without extra thoughts making it more intense.

SS   __/__/__

FEELINGS CHALLENGE: ANGRY ICE

Get a cup of ice cubes and go outside. Throw them as hard as you can at the ground. How does doing so make you feel?

5 MINUTES TO HAPPINESS

Step 1: Set a timer for 5 minutes and think about a positive memory.

Step 2: Notice what feelings come up alongside happiness.

Step 3: Try to remember as many details as you can in this memory (using all your senses, if possible).

Step 4: Leave this experience ready to notice details of happy moments throughout your day.

Write about a time you got into a disagreement with a friend. Did you understand their point of view? Did they understand yours? If there was resolution, how did it happen?

MTWTF   __/__/__

_____

_____

MTWTF   __/__/__

_____

_____

MTWTF   __/__/__

_____

_____

MTWTF   __/__/__

_____

_____

MTWTF   __/__/__

_____

_____

What does empathy mean to you? How is it different from sympathy?

SS ___/___/___

_____

_____

_____

_____

_____

_____

"Empathy is seeing with the eyes of another, listening with the ears of another, and feeling with the heart of another."

—Alfred Adler

Write about a time when a friend showed you empathy this week. How did it make you feel in that moment?

SS ___/___/___

_____

_____

_____

_____

_____

_____

FEELINGS CHALLENGE: HELPING HAND

Everyone could use a helping hand. Go tell a friend that you support them and ask how you can help them this week.

5 MINUTES TO EMPATHY

Step 1: Reflect on a difficult situation that a friend is going through.

Step 2: Think about how you would feel if you were in their shoes.

Step 3: Picture yourself supporting them. Notice what you are saying.

ACCEPTING OTHERS

It's one thing to accept friends; it's another to accept everyone. Think of someone you may not like and describe the feelings that come up when you think of them.

MTWTF ___/___/___

MTWTF ___/___/___

MTWTF ___/___/___

MTWTF ___/___/___

MTWTF ___/___/___

What do you need to do to accept people who are different from you?

SS   __/__/__

_____

_____

_____

_____

_____

_____

_____

"The opposite of anger is not calmness, it's empathy."

—Mehmet Oz

When we feel hurt or angry, it can affect our ability to empathize with others (even if they weren't the ones who hurt us). Discuss a difficult time you had communicating with someone and how you worked it out, or how empathy could've helped the situation.

SS   __/__/__

_____

_____

_____

_____

_____

_____

_____

FEELINGS CHALLENGE: PAY IT FORWARD!

Do something nice for someone you don't know. You can give them a sincere compliment, buy their lunch, or begin a conversation.

5 MINUTES TO EMPATHY

Step 1: Go to a public place and sit down.

Step 2: Notice the similarities between you and the people passing by. What might they be thinking and feeling?

Step 3: Without judgment, notice their body language, facial expressions, and words they might be saying.

Describe the ways you judge yourself and why you think you focus on those specific things.

MTWTF   __/__/__

MTWTF   __/__/__

MTWTF   __/__/__

MTWTF   __/__/__

MTWTF   __/__/__

Nonjudgmental stance (NJS) means looking at a situation and focusing only on the facts, without opinions. What are the differences between facts and opinions?

SS   __/__/__

"When we stop judging others and ourselves, our heart begins to open."

—Swami Dhyan Giten

Describe a challenging situation that happened this week. Then, rereading what you wrote, underline the opinions and circle the facts.

SS   __/__/__

FEELINGS CHALLENGE: AFFIRM FACTS

Write a fact-based affirmation on your mirror using a dry erase marker. Example: "I have friends and family who love me."

5 MINUTES TO CONFIDENCE

Step 1: Look at photos of models and describe what judgments come to mind.

Step 2: Now describe what you see based on facts (hair color, wardrobe, body posture).

Step 3: Notice the difference in the two ways of looking at things.

SELF-ACCEPTANCE

It can be difficult to truly accept yourself, but we all have great qualities. Write down one thing you like about yourself each day this week and explain why you like it.

MTWTF ___/___/___

_____

_____

MTWTF ___/___/___

_____

_____

MTWTF ___/___/___

_____

_____

MTWTF ___/___/___

_____

_____

MTWTF ___/___/___

_____

_____

What does it mean to accept yourself the way you are?

SS   __/__/__

_____

_____

_____

_____

_____

_____

_____

"The curious paradox is that when I accept myself just as I am, then I can change."

—Carl Rogers

Read the quote above. Do you think it's true that you need to accept yourself in order to change? Provide examples about why it is true or false.

SS   __/__/__

_____

_____

_____

_____

_____

_____

_____

Whenever you notice you are saying something critical or unkind to yourself, call a friend and tell them the facts of the situation. Remember, facts can be proven.

5 MINUTES TO HAPPINESS

Step 1: Choose a funny animal video that's about 5 minutes long.

Step 2: Focus only on the video as it's playing.

Step 3: Notice when you get distracted or your mind goes somewhere else, then refocus on the video.

CHALLENGING INSECURITY

Insecurities often show up when we are feeling envy, jealousy, or inferiority. Write about your insecurities. What is making you feel insecure? Notice if you are comparing yourself to others.

MTWTF ___/___/___

MTWTF ___/___/___

MTWTF ___/___/___

MTWTF ___/___/___

MTWTF ___/___/___

A good way to challenge insecurities is by stating your positive qualities. Identify three positive qualities about yourself and list examples.

SS _____/_____/_____

"You have been criticizing yourself for years, and it hasn't worked. Try approving of yourself and see what happens."

—Louise L. Hay

To challenge your insecurities, it can be helpful to see yourself as your own best friend. As if you were writing to a friend, write positive statements about yourself to replace negative thoughts about yourself.

SS _____/_____/_____

FEELINGS CHALLENGE: INTERVIEW A PARENT OR GUARDIAN!

Interview a parent or guardian about any insecurities they had when they were your age. Ask them how their insecurities affected them and how they learned to feel better about themself.

5 MINUTES TO CALM

Step 1: Find a quiet place to sit. Set a timer for 5 minutes and close your eyes.

Step 2: Picture yourself watching waves slowly crash into a rock. Listen to the sound the water makes as it comes up and then goes back to the ocean. Let your breathing align with the motion of the waves.

Step 3: Return to the present, awake and refreshed.

OREO: OBSERVE, REMEMBER, EXPERIENCE, LOVE

Using the Feelings Chart (pages viii and ix), *Observe* where you feel your emotions in your body. Rate their intensity from 0 to 10.

MTWTF   __/__/__

_____

_____

MTWTF   __/__/__

_____

_____

MTWTF   __/__/__

_____

_____

MTWTF   __/__/__

_____

_____

MTWTF   __/__/__

_____

_____

Think of the strongest emotions you feel right now, and, *Remember,* you are NOT your emotions. *Experience* them without trying to push them away. How do they make you feel in your body?

SS ___/___/___

"When awareness is brought to an emotion, power is brought to your life."
—Tara Meyer-Robson

Loving your emotion can be difficult, but every emotion has a function (a reason for showing up). Without judgment, write about the functions of your strongest emotions from this week.

SS ___/___/___

Go for a walk or a bike ride. As you look around, allow yourself to take in the wonder of how things were built or created. Think about the details.

5 MINUTES TO CALM

Step 1: Close your eyes. Notice which emotions you are feeling.

Step 2: Picture yourself sitting on a surfboard in the ocean surrounded by big waves. You can't stop the waves, but you can learn to surf them.

Step 3: Allow your breathing to be connected to the waves you are watching. Picture the waves as the strongest emotion you are feeling right now.

Step 4: Swim out to a wave and see yourself riding it all the way back to shore until it dissolves.

Write about a situation this week in which you used your strengths and how those qualities were helpful.

MTWTF   __/__/__

_____

_____

MTWTF   __/__/__

_____

_____

MTWTF   __/__/__

_____

_____

MTWTF   __/__/__

_____

_____

MTWTF   __/__/__

_____

_____

_____

Self-esteem comes from who we are, not just how we look, how athletic we are, or how popular we might be. Write about all the ways you are a good friend.

SS _____/_____/_____

_____

_____

_____

_____

_____

_____

_____

"If you are always trying to be normal, you will never know how amazing you can be."

—Maya Angelou

Things that make me unique are . . .

SS _____/_____/_____

_____

_____

_____

_____

_____

_____

_____

FEELINGS CHALLENGE: BE LOYAL!

Ask one of your friends or classmates about their goals or dreams for the future and what kind of support they need.

5 MINUTES TO GRATITUDE

Step 1: Set a timer for 3 minutes. Think of something or someone you dislike.

Step 2: Now, think of all the good things about it/them. Come up with as many "silver linings" as you can.

Step 3: Repeat steps 1 and 2 with qualities about yourself that you dislike. Be grateful for the silver linings you possess.

ACCOUNTABILITY

Accountability means taking ownership of your actions, and it can be difficult to do. Write down some ways that your parents or guardians help you stay accountable (e.g., waking you up for school or helping you eat healthy food).

MTWTF ___/___/___

MTWTF ___/___/___

MTWTF ___/___/___

MTWTF ___/___/___

MTWTF ___/___/___

Accountability for yourself and your actions is important if you want more independence. How were you accountable recently?

SS   __/__/__

"At the end of the day, we are accountable to ourselves. Our success is a result of what we do."

—Catherine Pulsifer

Identify and describe three things that you have succeeded at because you kept yourself accountable. An example would be acing a test you studied hard for.

SS   __/__/__

FEELINGS CHALLENGE: BE ACCOUNTABLE!

Set a goal of finishing a task or project this week. Make an accountability plan by using reminders or even recruiting a friend or family member to help.

5 MINUTES TO GRATITUDE

Step 1: Get a piece of paper and something to color with.

Step 2: Draw whatever emotions you are feeling right now.

Step 3: Spend time admiring your work. If your mind tries to judge the work, simply say, "I am noticing the positives right now," and go back to appreciating what you created.

DECISION-MAKING

Making good decisions takes practice, and it's important to think through decisions as often as possible. Write about some good decisions you made this week.

MTWTF ___/___/___

MTWTF ___/___/___

MTWTF ___/___/___

MTWTF ___/___/___

MTWTF ___/___/___

Make a pro/con list for a decision you need to make. On a scale from 0 to 10, rate each item by how important it is to you.

SS ___/___/___

"Emotions and reason are intertwined, and both are critical to problem solving."

—Antonio Damasio

Describe a problem you've had in the past or are having now. Brainstorm some solutions, even if they are outrageous, and then cross out the ones you decide won't work.

SS ___/___/___

FEELINGS CHALLENGE: WHO'S COOKING?!

Decide what you would like to eat for dinner one day this week, keeping everyone in your home in mind. Ask family members if your choice works for them. Then make or help make the dinner.

5 MINUTES TO CONFIDENCE

Step 1: Find a clear jar with a lid.

Step 2: Fill it with water, then add sand or dirt, glitter, and beads or small pebbles.

Step 3: Tighten the lid, shake the jar, and watch as everything slowly settles.

Step 4: Think about how your mind may get cloudy sometimes, and how a balance of logical and emotional thoughts can bring clarity and help you make positive decisions.

VALIDATING OTHERS

It's important to validate others' feelings. One way to do so is to listen actively and reflect—or repeat back—what people tell you. Write down something someone told you today and how they were feeling.

MTWTF   __/__/__

_____

_____

_____

MTWTF   __/__/__

_____

_____

_____

MTWTF   __/__/__

_____

_____

_____

MTWTF   __/__/__

_____

_____

_____

MTWTF   __/__/__

_____

_____

_____

Validation is showing you understand someone's point of view, emotions, and opinions about a situation. Write about a time this week when you helped someone feel heard.

SS   __/__/__

"Just like children, emotions heal when they are heard and validated."

—Jill Bolte Taylor

When you validate someone, how does it impact your relationship? How do you feel when you are validated?

SS   __/__/__

Replace the word "but" with the word "and" this week. For example, instead of saying "I have to study, but I'm too tired," say, "I have to study, and I'll need a snack so I can focus."

5 MINUTES TO HAPPINESS

Step 1: Close your eyes and picture a friend coming to you with a problem.

Step 2: Reflect (in your own words) what you heard them say and how you may have felt in their position.

Step 3: Tell your friend you understand where they're coming from, and compliment them on wanting to resolve their issue. Feel happy that you helped them feel better.

GIVE AND FAST

GIVE means to be **G**entle, **I**nterested, and **V**alidating and have an **E**asy manner. This helps people feel connected to you. Describe how you practiced GIVE today.

MTWTF   __/__/__

MTWTF   __/__/__

MTWTF   __/__/__

MTWTF   __/__/__

MTWTF   __/__/__

FAST (be **F**air, make no **A**pologies, **S**tick to your values, and be **T**ruthful) helps you gain respect. Describe how you can FAST today.

SS ___/___/___

_____

_____

_____

_____

_____

_____

"Be kind, be fair, be honest, be true, and all of these things will come back to you."

—Unknown

Imagine you have to deliver sad news to someone. What GIVE or FAST skills would you use?

SS ___/___/___

_____

_____

_____

_____

_____

_____

FEELINGS CHALLENGE: GIVE A COMPLIMENT!

Give a member of your household a sincere compliment!

5 MINUTES TO EMPATHY

Step 1: Think about your seven dimensions of culture (race, ethnicity, nationality, religion, gender, dis/ability, and age).

Step 2: Now picture yourself having a conversation with someone who has seven completely different cultural dimensions. What do you see yourself talking about?

Step 3: Try to picture yourself using GIVE during this conversation.

INDEPENDENCE VERSUS SUPPORT

Wanting independence while also needing support can be a challenge. Write about your experiences seeking independence and asking for support.

MTWTF ___/___/___

_____

_____

MTWTF ___/___/___

_____

_____

MTWTF ___/___/___

_____

_____

MTWTF ___/___/___

_____

_____

MTWTF ___/___/___

_____

_____

Too much independence can lead to trouble, and too much support can feel suffocating. Write about what a balance of the two would look like.

SS _/_/_

"Life is a balance of holding on and letting go."

—Rumi

Write about some independence you want, what responsibility you can take to show you are ready, and how your parents or guardians can support you.

SS _/_/_

FEELINGS CHALLENGE: NEW YOU!

Ask your parents or guardians for one new responsibility in exchange for one new thing you can do independently.

5 MINUTES TO CONFIDENCE

Step 1: Find a quiet place to sit and set a timer for 5 minutes.

Step 2: Observe your thoughts, without judgment, as if you were listening to an audiobook.

Step 3: Now, feel confident that you've enhanced your awareness of your own thoughts.

It is sometimes difficult to feel empathy for family because we can feel more hurt by family members than by outsiders. Write about a time a family member hurt your feelings and how you got through it.

MTWTF ___/___/___

MTWTF ___/___/___

MTWTF ___/___/___

MTWTF ___/___/___

MTWTF ___/___/___

What are your beliefs about your family relationships? Using a nonjudgmental stance, determine whether your beliefs are true.

SS ___/___/___

"Family is the place where acceptance and validation are most needed, but often the hardest to find."

—Bill Crawford

Family is important to our growth, but it can be hard for family members to validate us and vice versa. Write about a time this week when you felt understood by a family member.

SS ___/___/___

FEELINGS CHALLENGE: HELPING HAND

Offer to help a parent, guardian, or sibling with a chore.

5 MINUTES TO EMPATHY

Step 1: Choose a clip from a family video to watch for 5 minutes.

Step 2: Notice how family members might be feeling in the video.

Step 3: If you are able, ask them if your guesses were right.

PLEASE: PHYSICAL HEALTH, EATING, AVOID DRUGS/ALCOHOL, SLEEP, EXERCISE

List both your resources for and barriers to achieving **P**hysica**L** health goals.

MTWTF ___/___/___

_____

_____

_____

MTWTF ___/___/___

_____

_____

_____

MTWTF ___/___/___

_____

_____

_____

MTWTF ___/___/___

_____

_____

_____

MTWTF ___/___/___

_____

_____

_____

Eating healthy meals, **A**voiding drugs/alcohol, balanced **S**leep, and **E**xercising are so important to mental health. Identify which healthy habits you already have and how you practice them.

SS   __/__/__

_____

_____

_____

_____

_____

_____

"A good laugh and a long sleep are the best cures in the doctor's book."

—Irish Proverb

How does PLEASE impact your mood and stress? What's the best cure for when you're feeling stressed?

SS   __/__/__

_____

_____

_____

_____

_____

_____

FEELINGS CHALLENGE: PUSH PAUSE

Pick one thing you really like to do and pause doing it for three days (it's worth it!). This can improve appreciation of that activity and make you feel even happier afterward.

5 MINUTES TO HAPPINESS

Step 1: Find a quiet place and set a timer for 3 minutes.

Step 2: Picture yourself moving your body in a way that makes you happy.

Step 3: Allow yourself to notice your breathing and how good your body feels as you picture this movement.

Step 4: Once the timer goes off, stretch.

Self-soothing is what you do to help yourself calm down when you're upset. Write about something you do to self-soothe.

MTWTF   __/__/__

_____

_____

MTWTF   __/__/__

_____

_____

MTWTF   __/__/__

_____

_____

MTWTF   __/__/__

_____

_____

MTWTF   __/__/__

_____

_____

_____

Write down five songs that you can listen to when feeling sad or angry, and how they help you feel better.

SS   __/__/__

"If you close your eyes for just one minute, you can experience how a feeling or emotion is born, grows old, and passes away."

—Bhante Gunaratana

It can be helpful to experience an emotion in the moment, then let it pass. Write about a time you experienced a strong emotion and what you did to move past it.

SS   __/__/__

FEELINGS CHALLENGE: PET AN ANIMAL

Choose an animal to pet and (with permission from its owner) spend 10 minutes giving that animal attention. Notice how you feel.

5 MINUTES TO CALM

Step 1: Sit in your room and describe to yourself, in detail, five things you can see.

Step 2: Close your eyes and listen for four different sounds.

Step 3: Touch three things near you and describe their textures.

Step 4: Smell two things near you and taste one thing. Now take a deep breath and open your eyes.

WILLFULNESS VERSUS WILLINGNESS

Willfulness is expecting things around you to change but not wanting to accept or adapt to reality. What are some things in your life that are hard to accept? Why?

MTWTF ___/___/___

_____

_____

_____

MTWTF ___/___/___

_____

_____

_____

MTWTF ___/___/___

_____

_____

_____

MTWTF ___/___/___

_____

_____

_____

MTWTF ___/___/___

_____

_____

_____

Willingness means being open to thinking about experiences positively instead of negatively. It becomes easier with practice. Write about something you dislike that you wish you enjoyed doing.

SS   __/__/__

"Where the willingness is great, the difficulties cannot be great."

—Niccolò Machiavelli

Write about a difficult experience you had this week. How could doing the best with what you have help you in situations like this?

SS   __/__/__

FEELINGS CHALLENGE: SILVER LININGS!

Silver linings are positive parts of a bad situation. For example, maybe you missed the bus but had a great conversation with a friend while waiting for the next bus. Anytime you feel frustrated or upset about something you can't control, find a silver lining.

5 MINUTES TO HAPPINESS

Step 1: Find a quiet place to sit and set a timer for 5 minutes.

Step 2: Think about a challenge in your life and picture it as a cloud hanging over you.

Step 3: Focus on the cloud. With every breath you take, notice light shining from behind the cloud. The more you focus, the more you notice the light.

Step 4: Once time is up, notice how much lighter your challenge feels.

TIME BOUNDARIES

Your time is important, and you can decide how to spend it. What things do you want to spend time doing? Why do you love doing them?

MTWTF   __/__/__

_____

_____

MTWTF   __/__/__

_____

_____

MTWTF   __/__/__

_____

_____

MTWTF   __/__/__

_____

_____

MTWTF   __/__/__

_____

_____

How does it feel when you have to do things you don't want to do?

SS ___/___/___

"Balance is not better time management, but better boundary management."

—Betsy Jacobson

Write about a time when you felt comfortable saying "no" when someone wanted you to do something or how you compromised. How did it feel?

SS ___/___/___

FEELINGS CHALLENGE: PLAN YOUR TIME!

Plan an afternoon with a friend, and be sure to tell your parents or guardians all the details before you go (their time is important, too).

5 MINUTES TO GRATITUDE

Step 1: Close your eyes and picture your daily routine.

Step 2: Notice what things you have a responsibility to take care of, and what things are "extras."

Step 3: Picture yourself spending your day doing the things that are important to you and saying no to the things that aren't.

Step 4: Be grateful that you have the ability to say no to the extras.

JUST ACT

Often we think too much before doing something and then talk ourselves out of doing it. Write about something you wanted to do but didn't.

MTWTF ___/___/___

_____

_____

_____

MTWTF ___/___/___

_____

_____

_____

MTWTF ___/___/___

_____

_____

_____

MTWTF ___/___/___

_____

_____

_____

MTWTF ___/___/___

_____

_____

_____

"Just Act" is a way of overcoming procrastination by telling yourself, "This is what I'm going to do today" and then doing it! Write about something you were able to get done this week.

SS   __/__/__

"No one is free from something: something will surely be the reasons for our actions!"

—Ernest Agyemang Yeboah

Write about the thoughts that keep you from accomplishing your daily goals. What can you do to overcome those thoughts?

SS   __/__/__

FEELINGS CHALLENGE: JUST ACT!

Practice Just Act by noticing what is keeping you from getting things done. Give yourself 1 to 2 minutes to think about what you need in order to do something, then begin!

5 MINUTES TO CONFIDENCE

Step 1: Sit in a quiet place and visualize yourself doing a task.

Step 2: Focus on your breathing as your lungs fill with air, then release your breath. Imagine yourself achieving your task.

Step 3: When your mind brings up obstacles, instead of ignoring them, accept that they exist and see yourself overcoming them.

ALL OR NOTHING THINKING

Sometimes we think about things as one way or another. There are more than two single truths for any situation. Write about a time when you noticed the "shades of gray."

MTWTF   __/__/__

_____

_____

MTWTF   __/__/__

_____

_____

MTWTF   __/__/__

_____

_____

MTWTF   __/__/__

_____

_____

MTWTF   __/__/__

_____

_____

_____

"If I can't be perfect, why bother?" What do you think about this statement? Do you relate to it?

SS   __/__/__

_____

_____

_____

_____

_____

_____

"Giving up on your goal because of one setback is like slashing your other three tires because you got one flat."

—Unknown

Identify in-betweens to overcome all-or-nothing thinking. Instead of, "I'll never be good at math," think, "I could improve my math grade if I got extra help." How can you find more in-betweens?

SS   __/__/__

_____

_____

_____

_____

_____

_____

FEELINGS CHALLENGE: BE AGREEABLE!

For one day, try to agree in some way with everything someone says. For example, say "I might not wear that outfit, but it looks great on you!" when you don't like a particular outfit.

5 MINUTES TO HAPPINESS

Step 1: Take a seat in your room and choose an object to focus on.

Step 2: Visualize the space and where that object might fit and look good.

Step 3: Notice how many places it could possibly go (there is no "right" answer).

Step 4: Use this exercise to remember that there are often many options in life.

COMMUNICATION BOUNDARIES

Boundaries are important because they reduce the likelihood that you'll be hurt by others. Write down some things people say that hurt you. What boundaries can you set to prevent that from happening again?

MTWTF ___/___/___

_____

_____

_____

MTWTF ___/___/___

_____

_____

_____

MTWTF ___/___/___

_____

_____

_____

MTWTF ___/___/___

_____

_____

_____

MTWTF ___/___/___

_____

_____

_____

Boundaries are rules you set for yourself, not others. Write down your thoughts about this statement: "I have the right to say no." Do you feel comfortable saying no?

SS   __/__/__

"Communication works for those who work at it."

—John Powell

"If they never text me back, I know I am not a priority for them, and I will no longer prioritize them." This is an example of a communication boundary. Write about a time you set a communication boundary.

SS   __/__/__

In one week, see how many things you can say no to (within reason). Being confident saying "no" will help you do so more easily when faced with situations that feel uncomfortable or unhealthy for you. If you get at least three, treat yourself to some extra "me time."

5 MINUTES TO CONFIDENCE

Step 1: Sit with a good friend. Explain washing your hair to them as if they have never done it.

Step 2: Focus on all the details (not just "pour the shampoo and rub it on your hair").

Step 3: Ask your friend to explain how to tie a shoe and see if they miss any details.

Step 4: Reflect on how this helped you communicate effectively.

Knowing how and when to use social media helps us create healthy boundaries. What are you comfortable posting on social media?

MTWTF   __/__/__

_____

_____

MTWTF   __/__/__

_____

_____

MTWTF   __/__/__

_____

_____

MTWTF   __/__/__

_____

_____

MTWTF   __/__/__

_____

_____

Many people can see our social media (teachers, parents). Write down some information you may not want them to know.

SS   __/__/__

"To be yourself in a world that is constantly trying to make you something else is the greatest accomplishment."

—Ralph Waldo Emerson

People post what they want you to see, even if it doesn't reflect reality. This can impact our mood and raise our insecurities. How does social media impact you?

SS   __/__/__

FEELINGS CHALLENGE: OFF THE GRID!

Take three days off from all social media. Notice how your body and mind feel after three days.

5 MINUTES TO HAPPINESS

Step 1: Go for a walk.

Step 2: Notice how many sounds you hear (e.g., birds, wind, car horns).

Step 3: Think about how the sounds connect to so many lives or activities outside of your own.

Step 4: You miss a lot when focused on technology. It's okay to take a break!

LABELING

Labeling is when we attach names to things, even when they're wrong. For example, we might think, *"I am a loser"* or *"My parents are unfair."* Write about situations in which you have labeled yourself or someone else. Consider another way to look at people or events.

MTWTF   __/__/__

_____

_____

MTWTF   __/__/__

_____

_____

_____

MTWTF   __/__/__

_____

_____

MTWTF   __/__/__

_____

_____

MTWTF   __/__/__

_____

_____

How do you think labeling hurts you? Describe some ways you can prove a negative label to be untrue.

SS   __/__/__

_____

_____

_____

_____

_____

_____

"We spend a lot of time judging ourselves harshly for feelings that we had no role in summoning. The only thing you can control is how you handle it."

—Dan Harris

It's okay to experience an emotion without becoming that emotion. List some positive things you can tell yourself instead.

SS   __/__/__

_____

_____

_____

_____

_____

FEELINGS CHALLENGE: IDENTIFY YOURSELF!

We all have different roles we play in our lives (e.g., sibling, friend, student). Give each of your roles a name and pick a game to play, such as "Among Us," and be a different "you" each round.

5 MINUTES TO CALM

Step 1: Close your eyes and focus on each part of your body for a few seconds, starting at the top of your head and ending at the tip of your toes.

Step 2: Notice where you have good feelings, stress, or tension.

Step 3: Take a deep breath in and visualize all of the stress coming to your throat, then, when you exhale, blow it all out.

Being mindful means slowing down your thoughts and paying attention to the small things. Write down the details of what you remember about the past 24 hours.

MTWTF   __/__/__

_____

_____

MTWTF   __/__/__

_____

_____

MTWTF   __/__/__

_____

_____

MTWTF   __/__/__

_____

_____

MTWTF   __/__/__

_____

_____

On a separate piece of paper, write down something you would like to let go of. Fill a sink with water and place the paper underwater, then watch the ink wash away. Describe what doing so feels like.

SS   __/__/__

_____

_____

_____

_____

_____

_____

"Mindfulness is a way of befriending ourselves and our experience."

—Jon Kabat-Zinn

Pick an encouraging statement to write to yourself, such as "I am worthy." Write this five times with your nondominant hand, noticing any frustration or judgment, then releasing it.

SS   __/__/__

_____

_____

_____

_____

_____

_____

FEELINGS CHALLENGE: BE MINDFUL!

Watch your favorite show and notice the details, such as the colors of the actors' clothes or the sets. Then see if you can tell when the actors improvise their scripts.

5 MINUTES TO CALM

Step 1: Choose two colors: one to breathe in (healing), and one to breathe out (stress).

Step 2: Close your eyes and picture yourself slowly breathing in the healing color, and then slowly releasing the stressful color.

Step 3: Repeat this for 5 minutes, and see how refreshed and rejuvenated you feel.

Reviewing a past situation can help you understand it and may reduce future hurts. Think of a situation that caused you frustration or hurt, and write down your feelings about it.

MTWTF ___/___/___

MTWTF ___/___/___

MTWTF ___/___/___

MTWTF ___/___/___

MTWTF ___/___/___

You cannot control others, but you can control yourself. Write down what you noticed about yourself in the situations you wrote about. How did your body feel? What words did you use?

SS   __/__/__

"Chains of habit are too light to be felt until they are too heavy to be broken."

—Warren Buffett

Reviewing the situations you described, how could you have done things differently to possibly reach a different outcome? What might you do next time you find yourself in a similar situation?

SS   __/__/__

FEELINGS CHALLENGE: DO IT DIFFERENTLY!

Pick a genre of music that you haven't listened to before (or don't listen to often), and listen to it for three days. Try to figure out why other people might like it.

5 MINUTES TO EMPATHY

Step 1: Set a timer for 5 minutes. Close your eyes and picture yourself and a clone of you walking in a park.

Step 2: Try not to judge the conversation you are having with your clone; just notice what comes up and try to befriend your clone.

Step 3: Once the 5 minutes end, continue to be your own friend, giving good advice and validating your feelings.

We all feel sad sometimes, but some people feel sad often. Write about your experience with sadness and how it affects your relationships with other people.

MTWTF   __/__/__

_____

_____

_____

MTWTF   __/__/__

_____

_____

_____

MTWTF   __/__/__

_____

_____

_____

MTWTF   __/__/__

_____

_____

_____

MTWTF   __/__/__

_____

_____

_____

Sadness can impact our motivation and self-esteem and make us second-guess how people feel about us. Write about why sadness is an important emotion to experience and how it might help you.

SS _/_/_

_____

_____

_____

_____

_____

_____

"Sometimes it takes sadness to know happiness, noise to appreciate silence, and absence to value presence."

—Unknown

Write about ways you help yourself feel better when you are feeling sad. Why do you think those strategies help you?

SS _/_/_

_____

_____

_____

_____

_____

_____

FEELINGS CHALLENGE: CLEAN UP!

Walk around your neighborhood with a trash bag and gloves and pick up trash. Exercising and doing good deeds are great ways to increase happiness!

5 MINUTES TO HAPPINESS

Step 1: Close your eyes and picture something that made you feel sad. Notice what happens in your body as you do this.

Step 2: Inhale through your nose for 4 counts.

Step 3: Notice the tension build up in your body as you hold your breath for 4 counts.

Step 4: Exhale, slowly, for 8 counts, releasing all of the tension and stress that built up. Allow yourself to relax.

SETTING BOUNDARIES

Setting a boundary means being clear and direct about what you need. For example, "If you continue to talk to me disrespectfully, I will leave." Describe an important boundary you've set.

MTWTF ___/___/___

_____

_____

MTWTF ___/___/___

_____

_____

MTWTF ___/___/___

_____

_____

MTWTF ___/___/___

_____

_____

MTWTF ___/___/___

_____

_____

Guilt plays a big role in why we don't keep boundaries we have set. For example, we might think the boundary will hurt someone's feelings. Do you struggle with keeping boundaries? Why or why not?

SS ___/___/___

"Love yourself enough to set boundaries . . . You teach people how to treat you by deciding what you will and won't accept."

—Anna Taylor

Describe a situation in which you had to set a clear boundary and how it helped you.

SS ___/___/___

FEELINGS CHALLENGE: MY OPINION MATTERS

Disagree, assertively, with someone's opinion. Being assertive means standing up for your thoughts while having empathy for the other person's point of view.

5 MINUTES TO CONFIDENCE

Step 1: Visualize yourself at the bottom of a mountain that you have to climb.

Step 2: See yourself climbing and overcoming any obstacles that get in your way.

Step 3: Notice what you used inside of you to overcome the obstacles. Now you can go climb your own metaphorical mountains.

"I" statements are a great way to communicate your needs without blaming. "I feel <u>hurt</u> when <u>you don't text back</u> because <u>I feel that you don't care about me</u>." Fill in the blanks with situations and feelings you have experienced.

MTWTF ___/___/___

MTWTF ___/___/___

MTWTF ___/___/___

MTWTF ___/___/___

MTWTF ___/___/___

Communication becomes more difficult when we are angry. Write about a difficult situation you were able to get through with positive communication.

SS ___/___/___

_____

_____

_____

_____

_____

_____

"Good communication is the bridge between confusion and clarity."

—Nat Turner

Pauses are 10- to 30-minute breaks that help us gather our thoughts so we can clearly communicate. Write about a time when a pause helped you.

SS ___/___/___

_____

_____

_____

_____

_____

_____

FEELINGS CHALLENGE: GRAB A PILLOW

Take a pillow and hit it on the bed as hard as you can, very fast, for 1 minute. How do you feel afterward?

5 MINUTES TO EMPATHY

Step 1: Find a quiet place to sit, set a timer for 5 minutes, and close your eyes.

Step 2: Picture yourself sitting across from someone you love. Feel their presence around you.

Step 3: With every inhale, breathe in their loving-kindness and feel it run through your body. With every exhale, breathe out the same feelings they gave you, giving back to them.

CHECK AND REFLECT

Use this section to keep track of the Feelings Challenges and 5-Minute Mindfulness Moments you have done, and reflect on what those experiences were like for you. Did they work? What did you like best about the process? What could you have done differently? Next is a checklist where you can check off all 105 challenges and mindfulness moments as you do them, plus additional pages where you can write about your experiences. Some of them are tough, but so worth it, so just remember, You've Got This!

FEELINGS CHALLENGES

☐ Notice the Feelings!

☐ Show Gratitude!

☐ Get Connected!

☐ Get Motivated!

☐ Be Wise!

☐ Tally the Thoughts!

☐ De-trigger!

☐ Get Ready for Bed!

☐ Feel the Music!

☐ Eat Up!

☐ Blow Bubbles!

☐ Creative Exercise!

☐ Make a Vision Board!

☐ Beauty and the Filter

☐ Do It for YOU!

☐ "Way to Go" List

☐ Be Mindful

☐ Get the Patterns!

☐ Extra Time!

☐ Something New

☐ Should You?

☐ Trust and Secrets

☐ Be Creative!

☐ Knight in . . . Armor

☐ Angry Ice

☐ Helping Hand

☐ Pay It Forward!

☐ Affirm Facts

☐ Nothing but Facts!

☐ Interview a Parent or Guardian!

☐ Wow Yourself

☐ Be Loyal!

☐ Be Accountable!

☐ Who's Cooking?!

☐ Take the "But" out!

☐ Give a Compliment!

☐ New You!

☐ Helping Hand

☐ Push Pause

☐ Pet an Animal

☐ Silver Linings!

- ☐ Plan Your Time!
- ☐ Just Act!
- ☐ Be Agreeable!
- ☐ Say No!
- ☐ Off the Grid!
- ☐ Identify Yourself!

- ☐ Be Mindful!
- ☐ Do It Differently!
- ☐ Clean Up!
- ☐ My Opinion Matters
- ☐ Grab a Pillow

5-MINUTE MINDFULNESS MOMENTS

5 Minutes to Happiness

5 Minutes to Calm

Use the following pages to continue journaling about your experiences with the Feelings Challenges and 5-Minute Mindfulness Moments you completed. Simply write in the line which activity you are journaling about, note the date you finished it, and journal away.

_____ **PERFORMED ON** ___/___/___
(Challenge or Moment)

_____
_____
_____
_____
_____
_____
_____
_____

_____ **PERFORMED ON** ___/___/___
(Challenge or Moment)

_____
_____
_____
_____
_____
_____
_____

_____ **PERFORMED___/___/___**
(Challenge or Moment)

_____ **PERFORMED___/___/___**
(Challenge or Moment)

_____ **PERFORMED __/__/__**
(Challenge or Moment)

_____

_____

_____

_____

_____

_____

_____

_____

_____

_____

_____

_____

_____

_____ **PERFORMED __/__/__**
(Challenge or Moment)

_____

_____

_____

_____

_____

_____

_____

_____

_____

_____

_____

_____

_____

_____ **PERFORMED**___/___/___
(Challenge or Moment)

_____
_____
_____
_____
_____
_____
_____
_____
_____
_____
_____
_____
_____

_____ **PERFORMED**___/___/___
(Challenge or Moment)

_____
_____
_____
_____
_____
_____
_____
_____
_____
_____
_____
_____
_____

_____ **PERFORMED__/__/__**
(Challenge or Moment)

_____
_____
_____
_____
_____
_____
_____
_____
_____
_____
_____
_____
_____

_____ **PERFORMED__/__/__**
(Challenge or Moment)

_____
_____
_____
_____
_____
_____
_____
_____
_____
_____
_____
_____
_____
_____

_____ **PERFORMED** __/__/__

(Challenge or Moment)

_____ **PERFORMED** __/__/__

(Challenge or Moment)

_____ **PERFORMED**___/___/___
(Challenge or Moment)

_____ **PERFORMED**___/___/___
(Challenge or Moment)

_____ **PERFORMED** __/__/__
(Challenge or Moment)

_____

_____

_____

_____

_____

_____

_____

_____

_____

_____

_____

_____

_____

_____ **PERFORMED** __/__/__
(Challenge or Moment)

_____

_____

_____

_____

_____

_____

_____

_____

_____

_____

_____

_____

_____

_____ **PERFORMED**__/__/__
(Challenge or Moment)

_____

_____

_____

_____

_____

_____

_____

_____

_____

_____

_____

_____

_____

_____ **PERFORMED**__/__/__
(Challenge or Moment)

_____

_____

_____

_____

_____

_____

_____

_____

_____

_____

_____

_____

_____

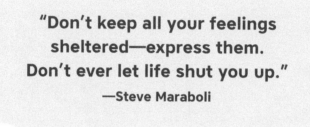

"Don't keep all your feelings
sheltered—express them.
Don't ever let life shut you up."
—Steve Maraboli

About the Author

 ***Tiffany Ruelaz, PhD, LPC, CDBT,*** is a community psychologist and licensed relational and trauma therapist who is passionate about helping teens find balance in their lives. As a certified DBT therapist, she uses mindfulness and emotion regulation skills to help people feel confident and comfortable with themselves. She is the director of CHANGE AZ, a nonprofit organization that helps people recover from trauma and provides therapy services to people living in rural areas. She lives with her husband, teen and pre-teen daughters, and two dogs, and she has a lot of experience challenging and accepting all the feelings.

CPSIA information can be obtained
at www.ICGtesting.com
Printed in the USA
JSHW011236160222
22986JS00011B/41